Original title:
Laughing in the Lightyear

Copyright © 2025 Creative Arts Management OÜ
All rights reserved.

Author: William Hawthorne
ISBN HARDBACK: 978-1-80567-878-6
ISBN PAPERBACK: 978-1-80567-999-8

The Brightness of our Delight

Bubbles float in cosmic streams,
As stardust winks with playful beams.
Galaxies giggle, swirling in tease,
Comets scoff, zipping with ease.

Planets spin with glee so grand,
Tickled by waves of laughter's band.
In this space where joy ignites,
We dance through days and endless nights.

Celestial Chuckles in the Void

Between the stars, a chuckle bounces,
Celestial bodies swap funny pounces.
A moonscape shimmers, with cheesy grins,
As asteroids joke, where bliss begins.

The universe tickles with cosmic jest,
Bringing whimsy to its very best.
With each twinkling flash, a giggle flows,
In the blackness, joy overflows.

Radiant Revelry Among the Planets

Oh, what fun among the spheres,
Planetary pals toast with cheers.
Jupiter jests, while Saturn sways,
In a raucous dance that sparks our rays.

The sun beams bright, a playful tease,
While meteors chase with grace and ease.
Down below, on Earth we sigh,
As stars wink back, vibrating high.

Whimsical Wonders of the Night Sky

Galactic giggles fill the night,
With shooting stars that flirt and bite.
A nebula clouds a joyful grin,
While comets laugh as they spin.

Wonders twirl in this boundless sea,
A wacky dance of jubilee.
Every twinkle tells a joke,
In this realm where dreams evoke.

Laughter in the Ether

Stars twinkle in a cosmic dance,
As comets slide with cheeky prance.
Nebulae giggle, sending a wink,
In space where all our dreams can sink.

Planets spin in merry delight,
Holding secrets, day and night.
A supernova bursts in a grin,
While galaxies chuckle, let the fun begin.

Sunshine in Spiral Arms

In the arms of spirals, joy does twirl,
A radiant sunbeam in a swirly whirl.
Asteroids blast through the joyful haze,
While moons bounce around in playful ways.

Cosmic rays tickle the surface bright,
And laughter echoes through the night.
Amongst the stars, we dance with grace,
In the endless vast, a joyful space.

Galactic Glee

Meteors race in a silly run,
Chasing each other, oh what fun!
In the void, a giggle resounds,
As starlight stretches and asteroids bound.

Wormholes twist in a playful leap,
Through interstellar dreams they creep.
In the vastness, joy expands,
While the universe claps with unseen hands.

Echoes of Cosmic Laughter

Echoes ripple through the grand expanse,
With every star, the cosmos prance.
Whispers of joy float in the night,
Every twinkle adds to the light.

Galaxies spin with a jovial cheer,
Cosmic chortles ringing near.
In the stillness of space, they play,
While the universe smiles, come what may.

Witty Wonders Among the Stars

Twinkling tales in the cosmic breeze,
A comet slips, tickling the trees.
Planets giggle in a dance of light,
While asteroids chuckle, oh, what a sight!

Galaxies swirl in a teasing spin,
Milky Way whispers where fun begins.
Supernovae burst with colors so bright,
Making wishes on starlit night!

Jovial Journeys

Rockets zoom with a playful cheer,
Cosmic clowns in the atmosphere.
Shooting stars sprinkle giggles and glee,
As they race past a laughing tree.

Meteor showers drop jokes with flair,
While space cats frolic without a care.
Aliens dance with all their might,
Underneath the moon's soft light!

Nebula Nonsense

In a cloud of colors, laughter erupts,
Silly sounds from where stardust cups.
Funny shapes in the swirling bright,
Make even the comets chuckle with delight.

Pulsars pulse with a rhythmic jest,
Echoing grins from the cosmic crest.
Every nova plays a playful tune,
As planets play tag beneath the moon!

Quasar Jokes

Quasars beam with a radiant glow,
Telling tales of the cosmic show.
Galactic giggles twinkle and sing,
Inviting laughter on a shining wing.

Stars whisper secrets of jokes untold,
In a universe vast, and bright, and bold.
Light-years stretch with a cheerful chime,
In the endless dance of space and time!

Cosmic Capers

Stars twinkle like eyes, so bright,
Planets dance in cosmic delight.
Asteroids waltz with a giggling swoop,
While comets join in a merry loop.

With each twirl and tumble, they play,
Creating mischief in a grand ballet.
The moon grins wide, a cheeky sight,
As stardust sprinkles the endless night.

The Whimsy of the Universe

Galaxies giggle in swirling hues,
Space critters play hopscotch in new shoes.
A nebula chuckles as it spins around,
While whimsical rockets make silly sounds.

Black holes tease with a playful swirl,
Inviting all comets to give it a whirl.
Astro-kittens chase beams of light,
Frolicking freely in the starry night.

Dawn of Galactic Giggles

The sun peeks in with a beam of cheer,
Whispering jokes for all to hear.
Solar flares wave like flags in a race,
While the planets clap with glee and grace.

Amidst the stardust, a ruckus ensues,
Space pirates jive in outlandish shoes.
A meteor shower, a sparkling show,
Brings about chuckles, the galaxy's glow.

Intergalactic Joyride

Spaceships zoom like laughter on the run,
Through loops and spirals, they spin and run.
Twirling past moons with a jovial cheer,
Echoing giggles that all can hear.

Alien friends share a hearty jest,
With a cosmic feast, they're at their best.
Asteroids serve up a delicious pie,
As laughter echoes from the stars up high.

Harmony of the Heavens

Stars twinkle like eyes, in a cosmic dance,
Galaxies spin, giving rhythm a chance.
Asteroids wobble, all dressed up bright,
Jovial comets, racing through the night.

Planets in tune, with a chuckle and spin,
Orbiting joy, where the giggles begin.
Nebulas swirl in a colorful show,
Painting the cosmos with humor aglow.

Meteor showers bring laughter anew,
Shooting through space, as if just for you.
Every twinkle and wink, a jest from afar,
The universe chuckles, beneath every star.

In a realm where the silly meets sublime,
Every echoing giggle transcends space and time.
Let's dance with the moons, as we join the delight,
In a symphony glowing, through the canvas of night.

Radiance and Revels

In the heart of the cosmos, a party takes flight,
With pulsars whispering jokes, softer than light.
Photons are frolicking, bouncing on beams,
Shiny and cheerful, they burst with our dreams.

Supernova explosions, the life of the bash,
Sparkling confetti in a colorful splash.
Gravity's tug isn't heavy tonight,
As laughter floats freely, shining so bright.

Solar flares flicker with mischievous grace,
Winking like children in this vast, open space.
Each twinkling star shares a cosmic tale,
Of merry adventures that always prevail.

Jovial echoes through celestial halls,
With giggles and grins, as the universe calls.
In the warmth of this laughter, let joy brightly swell,
A cosmic jubilee, where we all can dwell.

Tidal Waves of Laughter

Waves of our joy crash, an infinite sea,
With bubbles of giggles, wild and carefree.
The tides rise and fall, in a grand, silly spree,
All dancing together, just you and me.

Echoing ripples of humor abound,
In each playful motion, pure magic is found.
From the depths of the cosmos, laughter unfurls,
Carried on currents that twist and that twirl.

Sparkling moonbeams, like friends lost at night,
Chase shadows away with their shimmering light.
The galaxies shimmer in a whimsical trance,
While stars sway together, inviting a dance.

With a flip and a splash, we ride through the glee,
Creating a ruckus, just boundless and free.
In this space of pure fun, where laughter's a wave,
We'll surf through the cosmos, forever, so brave.

Smiles on Solar Winds

Breezes of joy from the sun that we feel,
Carry our laughter, like a cosmic wheel.
With every gust, a tickle of cheer,
Flowing through stardust, making fun clear.

Whirling like leaves, in a playful ballet,
Galactic gales chase our worries away.
Dreams on the flurry, with giggles entwined,
The universe smiles, in each twist it designed.

A ride on the rays, with a wink and a grin,
As space-time wraps us in joy from within.
Bright comets sail by, like jokes in the sky,
Reminding us always, to laugh and to fly.

So let's soar together on winds full of smiles,
With laughter that echoes across light-years' miles.
In the embrace of the cosmos, we dance without care,
With joy as our compass, forever we share.

Silliness in the Stellar Sea

Bubbles pop in cosmic fun,
Dancing stars, oh what a run!
Giggles twirl in the milky hue,
Wobbling moons in a silly queue.

Planets spin with a chuckle loud,
Asteroids stray from their proud cloud.
Wishing stars wink with glee,
Waving hands from the zany sea.

Euphoric Echoes Beneath Distant Suns

Silly whispers from the sun,
Shadows play, just for fun.
Comets race in merry flight,
Tickling beams of vibrant light.

Laughter bubbles from afar,
Echoes dance where dreams are.
Stardust snickers, twinkling bright,
In the mirthful cosmic night.

Cosmic Bliss in the Vast Expanse

Jovial clouds in playful chase,
Swirling joy in boundless space.
Shooting stars wear goofy grins,
Whirling wonders where fun begins.

Nebulas purr with delight so bold,
Jests unfold in shades of gold.
Galaxies giggle, twists and turns,
As the universe cheerfully burns.

Sprightly Spirits in a Celestial Ambience

Sprightly sprites in twinkling haze,
Bouncing light in wondrous ways.
Joyous beams leap and glide,
Cheerful dreams, they cannot hide.

Nebulae shimmer with gleeful cheer,
Spinning tales of fun, sincere.
With jolly hearts, they float and sway,
In the cosmic game of play.

Orbiting Amusement

In a spaceship made of cheese,
We fly past stars with ease,
Comets play a silly tune,
Bouncing with the light of the moon.

Asteroids dance a wobbly jig,
Wormholes twist, oh, what a gig!
Galaxies giggle, can you believe?
In this space, we never grieve.

Planets wear their best attire,
A swirl of color, never tire,
Saturn's rings, a bright confetti,
In this orbit, we're all ready!

Shooting stars burst with delight,
Tickling planets in the night,
Cosmic chuckles fill the sky,
As we drift and soar, oh my!

Cascades of Cosmic Joy

A nebula blooms in splendid cheer,
Sprinkling laughter far and near,
Supernova confetti rains,
In every heart, joy remains.

Galactic games, a merry chase,
Joyrides through the cosmic space,
Astrological funny faces,
Bring smiles to all the right places.

Silly aliens tap dance around,
As astronauts flip and bound,
Twinkling stars poke fun at fate,
In this galaxy, we celebrate!

With cosmic bubbles and gleeful glee,
The universe is wild and free,
In every twirl, a hearty cheer,
Echoes of fun, loud and clear!

Twinkling Tricks of Time

Tick-tock, the time laughs loud,
As seconds dance, oh, what a crowd!
Hourglasses tumble, a funny sight,
While minutes pirouette, pure delight.

Chronicles hide in playful jest,
Where seconds slip away, not rest,
Calendars wink with a cheeky grin,
As laughter spills from deep within.

Eons wrap in goofy bows,
While paradoxes throw some shows,
Temporal pranks that twist and bend,
In the cosmos, fun has no end!

Hopping through the ages bright,
Joyous moments take their flight,
In every tick, a tale to tell,
Where giggles linger, all is well!

Ecstatic Echoes of Infinity

In a realm where echoes soar,
Boundless laughs forevermore,
Infinity sings with glee and play,
As galaxies twirl and sway.

Laughter ripples through the void,
Silly dreams we all enjoyed,
Joyful clowns on cosmic rides,
As stardust twinkles, fun abides.

Nebulas giggle, stars collide,
Crafting joy from every side,
Wonders burst like fireworks bright,
Creating magic in the night.

Galactic jesters make us beam,
In this grand and funny dream,
With buoyant spirits, we explore,
In infinity, we laugh and soar!

Comet's Comical Path

A comet zips on a silly spree,
With tail so bright, it tickles the sea.
Stars chuckle softly, a cosmic jest,
As it zooms past the moon, always the best.

Planets giggle, their belts all a-twirl,
While asteroids dance, as they spin and swirl.
The sky bursts with laughter, a joyful parade,
In this wacky universe, no moment's delayed.

A nebula fluffs, like cotton so grand,
As meteors throw a rock-n-roll band.
The black holes yawn in a playful mood,
Gobbling up humor, the cosmic food.

With space dust scattered and joy all around,
These comets and stardust refuse to be bound.
Through chuckles and giggles, they merrily race,
Creating a scene that's a warm, happy place.

Lightheartedness in the Abyss

In the depths where the dark shadows creep,
A smile emerges through silence so deep.
The stars whisper secrets of silly delight,
As they twinkle and wiggle in the cold, dark night.

Fish in the void do the silliest sleight,
Wobbling in rhythms that bring pure light.
Jellyfish chuckle, floating with ease,
Making waves of laughter that ripple like breeze.

Asteroids sing in a goofy refrain,
While black holes grin, never feeling the strain.
Wormholes waltz with a twist and a spin,
In this jolly abyss, where giggles begin.

With each flip of a comet, a chuckle rings out,
In this endless vastness, there's never a doubt.
The universe dances, where fun never fades,
In this lighthearted abyss, pure joy cascades.

Joyful Dances of the Planets

Round and round they go, a cosmic ballet,
Planets twirl and whirl, all night and day.
Venus brings the rhythm, while Jupiter sings,
A symphony of giggles, oh, what joy it brings.

Saturn's rings shine with laughter and glee,
Each spin and each twist, a sight to see.
Mars does a jig, with dust clouds that pout,
While Neptune spins jokes, leaving no doubt.

Mercury pops in with a cheeky grin,
Winking at Earth, let the fun begin!
Galaxies gather, a festival bright,
In the dance of the planets, everything's right.

With moons as their partners, they glide through space,
Creating a pattern of mirth and embrace.
In this winking waltz, under stardust so fine,
The joyful planets together align.

Celestial Cartwheels

Stars do cartwheels on a blanket of night,
Flipping and flopping, what a delightful sight!
The Milky Way giggles, a swirl of bright cheer,
As cosmic kites dance, with nothing to fear.

Planets take turns in their playful spins,
Each rotation a whirl, where the fun never thins.
When galaxies glide, they spark joy so grand,
In this tapestry woven by a laughing hand.

Astrological acrobats toss in the air,
With comets providing the laughter to share.
Orbits collide in a rhythm divine,
As heavenly bodies perform and entwine.

So under this dome, where the stars freely play,
Their giggling echoes have come out to stay.
In celestial realms, full of joy and of light,
Cartwheels keep spinning, from day into night.

Dancing Among Heavenly Bodies

In a swirl of cosmic dust, we spin,
Stars wink in rhythmic patterns, a grin.
Planets clink like glasses in a toast,
As we twirl, we giggle, our joy the most.

Galaxies giggle, a stellar parade,
With every twinkle, a jest is made.
We sway in silence, with laughter unbound,
In this waltz of wonders, delight is found.

Comets with tails, they race by in glee,
Their shimmering trails sparkle bright, you see.
We skip through stardust, a whimsical flight,
With each chuckle echoing through the night.

Orbiting moons throw a party so grand,
Their craters shaped like a friendly hand.
With meteors dancing, we join in the fun,
Under this cosmic carnival, we run.

Joyride Through the Milky Way

Strapped in a spaceship, laughter takes flight,
As we zoom past stars that twinkle so bright.
Asteroids giggle, give us a push,
Through cosmic giggles, in a galactic rush.

Whirling around black holes, we spin with delight,
Their swirling edges seem to invite.
We sing to the comets, our joy loud and clear,
In the twists and the turns, there's nothing to fear.

Nebulas bloom like a carnival's glow,
Their colors exploding, putting on a show.
As planets dance clumsily, clanging their tunes,
Echoes of chuckles bounce off the moons.

Our joyride through space feels endlessly free,
With stars all around, it's just you and me.
In the fabric of cosmos, our laughter resounds,
A timeless adventure where happiness abounds.

Starlit Serenades and Smiles

Under starry chandeliers, we twirl and sway,
Each twinkle a note in our serenade play.
Galactic giggles and rhythms align,
As we float on moonbeams, sipping space wine.

Planets hum softly, a joyful refrain,
While shooting stars dash like wild candy canes.
Our laughter entwined with the cosmos' embrace,
In this stellar concert, joy takes its place.

With shadows that dance in the light of the night,
Every ripple of laughter shines ever so bright.
Together we sing to the wonders above,
A melody woven with stardust and love.

In this night of mirth, with smiles all around,
The universe echoes a jubilant sound.
With every beat, our hearts skip a mile,
In this starlit serenade, we treasure each smile.

Glee Beyond the Nebulas

Beyond the bright clouds of shimmering hue,
We hop and we skip in the cosmic view.
Stars roll around, their laughter a spark,
In the vastness of space, we make our mark.

Nebulae wink with their playful embrace,
Whispers of joy in this boundless space.
Like children, we frolic on stellar swings,
With the tickling touch of the universe's strings.

As we dance through the void, our spirits take flight,
Galactic playgrounds in the veil of the night.
Each pirouette spins a new tale to tell,
In this zany adventure, we're under a spell.

Beyond swirling halos, we gather our cheer,
With each cosmic giggle, the universe hears.
In the laughter of night, we forever reside,
Bound together in joy, the stars as our guide.

Starlit Shenanigans

In a galaxy where giggles bloom,
Stars play pranks with a silly zoom.
Comets tickle the cosmic dust,
Laughter bounces with joyous thrust.

Planets spin in a wobbly dance,
Space cats frolic, they take the chance.
Meteor showers splash with glee,
As twinkling voices echo, whee!

Aliens wear shoes two sizes wide,
Tripping over beams with cosmic pride.
A supernova bursts out a grin,
Creating bursts of jokes within.

Through the void, the laughter streams,
Chasing dreams like vibrant beams.
Starlit mischief fills the air,
In this universe of playful flair.

Cosmic Chuckles

Giggling planets in a silly swirl,
Asteroids giggle as they twirl.
Space dust dances with a happy tune,
While moons play hide and seek with the noon.

A star sneezes, sending sparkles wide,
Creating laughter where shadows hide.
Silly comets with their fluffy tails,
Zoom past stargazers telling tales.

Neptune wears a polka dot hat,
While Jupiter beams, growing quite fat.
Cosmic critters burst out in song,
Filling the void where they all belong.

Galaxies swirl in joyous delight,
Chasing clouds that float in the night.
In a universe topped with fun,
Giggles echo 'neath a giant sun.

Bright Days in the Void

Vacuum echoes with joyous yells,
Spinning rockets ring like bells.
Galactic clowns on a comet ride,
Whizzing by with the stars as their guide.

Shooting stars play peek-a-boo,
As laughter paints the skies anew.
In this expanse where wonders meet,
Every twinkle feels like a treat.

Nebulas weave jokes in vibrant hues,
While shooting stars share silly news.
Quantum giggles tickle the air,
Creating fun from naught to spare.

Space-time pirouettes in pure delight,
Tickling fancies all through the night.
In a void where joy takes flight,
Every moment feels just right.

Celestial Jests

Under a blanket of sparkling dreams,
Cosmic jesters pull at moonbeams.
Planets chuckle at the sun's bright face,
While meteors race in a hilarious chase.

Witty whispers drift through the dark,
Echoes of laughter ignite a spark.
Galaxies giggle, swirling with ease,
Tickled by cosmic celestial breeze.

A lunar rabbit hops with a flair,
Joking with stars that sparkle and glare.
Halos of humor wrap all around,
As laughter echoes through the profound.

Constellations have secrets to share,
In their twinkling, they strand the air.
Joy in the universe we can't contain,
In celestial jesting, we dance in the rain.

Stellar Serenade

In the night, the stars peek through,
Funny shapes, a grand debut.
A comet wiggles, a planet spins,
Celestial dance, where joy begins.

Galactic whispers, laughter flows,
Asteroids tripping, oh how it glows.
Nebulas chuckle, bright and bold,
In cosmic play, a sight to behold.

Shooting stars wink, with a playful grin,
Each spark a joke, where giggles begin.
Orbiting moons in a jolly race,
Chasing the sun, with a comical face.

All around, in this vast expanse,
Celestial beings join in a dance.
With each tick of time, smiles align,
In the universe's heart, pure delight shines.

Laughter Beneath the Constellations

Under the arch of twinkling lights,
A cosmic party ignites the nights.
Dancing waves of giggles spread,
While constellations laugh overhead.

Planets wobble in humorous glee,
Orions do the twist, come see!
In the midst of stardust's swirl,
Joyful echoes begin to twirl.

Meteor showers rain down smiles,
As everyone plays hopscotch for miles.
Martians share a witty jest,
In comedic timing, they are blessed.

With each bright star, a chuckle shared,
Good humor floats, no one is spared.
Beneath the night, where spirits soar,
Every light beams laughter more and more.

Twinkling Tales of Mirth

Once in a sky of azure dreams,
Twinkling hopes burst at the seams.
Galaxies grinning, side by side,
In this universe, joy won't hide.

Black holes giggle, making a scene,
Silly antics, oh what a routine!
Supernova bursts with riotous cheer,
In the vast void, laughter draws near.

Pulsars pulse with a beat so bright,
Singing songs through the endless night.
Quasars beam with radiant laughs,
Telling stories of cosmic gaffes.

In this realm of mirth and jest,
Every shooting star is nature's best.
Come join the fun, let spirits lift,
In twinkling tales, we find our gift.

Galaxy's Giggle Fit

In the realm where starlight plays,
Fun and frolic weave through rays.
Planets chuckle in the milky mist,
Each orbit sways to a funny twist.

The cosmos brims with cheerful sights,
Bouncing comets, giggling lights.
Alien creatures crack fun-filled jokes,
While starry eyes twinkle, the universe pokes.

Astrological antics make folks grin,
As laughter bursts from within the spin.
Spacey silliness envelopes the night,
Ensuring every heart feels delight.

Join the dance, let spirits uplift,
In the galaxy's giggle, we find our gift.
A boundless joy, forever to share,
In the celestial laughter, we breathe fresh air.

Radiant Realms of Laughter

In the sky where giggles play,
Stars wink bright, come what may.
Comets race with silly grins,
Chasing dreams where joy begins.

Planets spin in a vibrant dance,
Mirthful moves, a cosmic chance.
Floating through this jester's maze,
We find cheer in endless ways.

Jokes rattle in a meteor's tail,
Cosmic chuckles tell the tale.
Nebulas burst with colors bright,
Painting smiles across the night.

With every twinkle, laughter's singed,
Eclipses mark when giggles cling.
In radiant realms, spirits soar,
Underneath a starlit roar.

Celestial Carnival

Gather 'round in the vast expanse,
Where stars twirl in a comical dance.
Galaxies twinkle with jokes to share,
Laughter spills into cosmic air.

A comet's tail, a slide of glee,
Orbiting joy, sweet jubilee.
Neon planets on carousel spin,
Spreading laughter, let the fun begin.

Asteroids juggle, making us smile,
Through stardust trails, we run a mile.
Witty quips echo from every sun,
In this carnival, we all are one.

Twinkling tickets, we hold so dear,
Rides of humor, no hint of fear.
Underneath this cosmic tent,
Life's a joke, and we're content.

Stellar Chortles

In night's embrace where whispers bloom,
The universe bursts with humor's zoom.
Planets giggle, their orbits sway,
In stellar chortles, night turns to day.

Asteroids play peek-a-boo,
Winking at us from the blue.
Supernovas pop with a grin,
Shooting sparks of joy within.

Black holes burp in a cosmic jest,
As laughter echoes through the quest.
Stars trip over each other's beams,
Creating a canvas filled with dreams.

With every flash, a chuckle wakes,
An interstellar joy that shakes.
Merriment rides on Saturn's rings,
Twirling, soaring, like endless flings.

Mirth in the Milky Way

Through the stretch of the galactic sea,
Mirth flows freely, wild and free.
Dancing dust in a carefree whirl,
Outrageous laughter begins to swirl.

Galaxies grin with a playful sway,
Tickling moons in a cheeky way.
Stars tease each other with playful bops,
In wild tales, the laughter never stops.

A cosmic game of hide and seek,
With giggles that echo, and laughter peaks.
Comets skate on laughter's beam,
As meteors burst like a vibrant dream.

In the heart of the stellar night,
Every twinkling wink feels so right.
Surrender to joy, don't delay,
Embrace the mirth in the Milky Way.

Stars Chuckle

In the night, the stars play,
Winking bright in their ballet.
They giggle in a cosmic whirl,
As planets twist and swirl.

Galaxies spin with glee,
Shooting stars race, wild and free.
Nebulas puff their colorful cheeks,
Creating laughter that brightly speaks.

Comets zoom with a bright tail,
Leaving a path of playful trail.
Each twinkle holds a joke untold,
In this universe, brave and bold.

So, gaze up high and find your cheer,
Join the dance, the stars appear.
In the vastness, joy ignites,
Cosmic chuckles fill the nights.

Joy Beyond the Horizon

Beyond the dawn, where dreams take flight,
A world awaits, so sunny and bright.
With silly clouds that tickle the sun,
Every moment is pure, joyous fun.

Laughter echoes through fields of green,
Where children play, so carefree and keen.
Butterflies flutter, join the spree,
Dancing on the breeze, wild and free.

The trees sway like they've heard a joke,
While rivers giggle as they provoke.
Joy lies hidden in every glance,
Inviting all to take a chance.

So chase the light, let shadows melt,
In this bright world, pure joy is felt.
With open hearts, we find our way,
Across the horizon, we'll laugh and play.

Laughter Across the Cosmos

In a realm where comets glance,
Galactic creatures start to dance.
Their chuckles echo through the night,
A symphony of pure delight.

Asteroids roll with a playful claim,
Claiming each star as their fame.
Floating through the sky so wide,
With a giggle, they try to hide.

Celestial jesters make their rounds,
Spreading joy in cosmic bounds.
With every twirl and every spin,
They cover the universe with a grin.

So join the fun and don't be shy,
Under the blanket of endless sky.
For in this void where silence reigns,
Laughter dances through the veins.

Grins of the Galaxy

In the arms of dusk, stars gleam,
With smiles that make the planets beam.
Each twinkle tells a story so sweet,
A merry dance, a cosmic treat.

Satellites whirl in a gleeful chase,
With giggles echoing in their race.
Galactic winds carry playful sighs,
While moonbeams wink from the darkened skies.

Pulsars beat like a joyful heart,
Sending waves of laughter that won't depart.
Black holes grin with mischievous flair,
At all the wonders floating in air.

So lift your gaze and join the show,
Where happiness floats, and star beams glow.
In this universe of endless cheer,
Grins of the galaxy draw us near.

Euphoria Across the Universe

In the void, a tickle wide,
Stars burst forth, full of pride.
Dancing comets spin and twist,
Cosmic giggles swirl in mist.

Asteroids bounce like children play,
Spinning tales of night and day.
Galaxies chuckle, shining bright,
In this vast, whimsical flight.

Planets wobble in merry glee,
As space dust laughs in jubilee.
Nebulas twirl in vibrant hues,
Sharing secrets, old and new.

In this cosmic carnival, we cheer,
Finding joy in all we hold dear.
Euphoria wraps us, a warm embrace,
In this endless, playful space.

Joyful Journeys among the Stars

Rockets zoom with silly grins,
Astronauts play, and space begins.
Wormholes wink with a cheeky light,
Transporting dreams through the night.

Jupiter laughs with a rumbling voice,
While Saturn twirls, it's a party of choice.
Constellations giggle in bright array,
Creating mischief, come what may.

Shooting stars take turns to race,
As stardust sprinkles across our face.
Each journey filled with whimsy and cheer,
In the universe, we lose our fear.

With every twist and every bend,
Friendship blossoms, hearts ascend.
Together we sail through cosmic streams,
Laughing aloud, chasing our dreams.

Lighthearted Dreams on a Starry Night

Underneath a blanket of twinkling lights,
We share our secrets, our funny sights.
Moonbeams chuckle, throwing shadows wide,
In this lighthearted night, we confide.

Dancing fireflies weave through the air,
Lighting up laughter, everywhere.
Planetary pals join the fun,
In this dreamy race, we all run.

Meteors tumble, creating a show,
While giggles escape as we stand in a row.
With every breeze, a new joke flies,
Boundless joy painted in our eyes.

As galaxies wink, we share a cheer,
In this embrace, we have no fear.
Lighthearted moments, pure delight,
Together we shine, a starry night.

Celestial Giggles in the Cosmos

In the cosmos where wonders unfold,
Celestial giggles, stories untold.
Stars whisper secrets in playful tones,
In this vast expanse, we're never alone.

Orbits waltz in a merry parade,
While black holes chuckle, unafraid.
Shooting stars set the night aglow,
With every laugh, our spirits grow.

Comets streak with sparkly trails,
Echoing joy in cosmic tales.
Galactic friends gather near,
Sharing smiles, spreading cheer.

So let us dance through the endless space,
In this universe, we find our place.
With every giggle, we ignite the night,
In celestial bliss, our hearts take flight.

Embracing the Cosmos with Cheer

In dazzling skies, we dance and twirl,
Stars wink at us, as dreams unfurl.
Galaxies swirl in a playful spree,
We jump with joy, wild and free.

A comet's tail brings a merry song,
Asteroids giggle, it won't be long.
Orbiting antics, a cosmic play,
Grins abound as we float away.

Lunar beams tickle our shining toes,
Secret jokes from the universe flows.
Between the planets, smiles ignite,
In the vast expanse, we find delight.

With every beam of a radiant star,
We chase the laughter, near and far.
Together we gather in jubilant flight,
Embracing the cosmos, hearts feeling light.

Stellar Laughter Unbound

In a nebula bright, we craft our fun,
Stars burst with glee, a cosmic run.
Planets spin tales, full of jest,
In this grand show, we are the best.

A quasar's wink sends us into fits,
Giggles echo from stardust bits.
With every orbit, we share a laugh,
Floating lightyears on our joyful path.

When meteors soar, we jump and cheer,
The universe whispers, 'Laughter is near!'
Gravity pulls us, but we float away,
In this endless dance, we seize the day.

We spin through space, what a delightful ride,
On waves of laughter, we joyfully glide.
A universe of chuckles, we find our place,
In the arms of the cosmos, we embrace.

Twinkling Hearts and Cosmic Jests

Twinkling stars share secrets so sweet,
Cosmic jesters, we take our seat.
Floating through galaxies, we laugh and play,
In this theater of night, we shout hooray!

Astro-antics fill our hearts with glee,
Comets sharing jokes, just you and me.
Laughter bursts forth, a supernova's glow,
In the cosmic circus, we steal the show.

Meteor showers rain joy from above,
Every sparkle twinkles, a joke we love.
Saturn's rings twirl with rhythmic grace,
In the dance of planets, we find our place.

With every giggle, space bends with cheer,
Together we journey, drawing friends near.
In the tapestry of stars, we twirl and jest,
In this wondrous space, we are truly blessed.

Chronicles of Joy in the Cosmos

In the vast expanse, we pen our tales,
With ink made of stardust, our laughter sails.
Nebulas burst with brilliant delight,
In this cosmic story, everything feels right.

Galactic giggles ripple through time,
Winking at moons, creating our rhyme.
With every heartbeat, the universe glows,
In the chronicles spun, our humor grows.

Satellites spin with a teasing flair,
Spinning around, without a care.
Planets chime in, a chorus so grand,
Together we'll dance, hand in hand.

With tales of joy, we weave the night,
Through swirling stars, our spirits take flight.
In this cosmic dance, we find our voice,
Embracing the joy, we jubilantly rejoice.

Happiness in the Heliosphere

In a land where sunbeams play,
Bouncing like a child at play,
Jokes fly high on solar wings,
Laughter's song is what joy brings.

With every twinkle, stars conspire,
To spread delight, a cosmic fire,
Bananas dance, and moons now spin,
In this realm, let's all dive in.

Meteor showers drop some pies,
As planets wobble, oh what a surprise!
Swinging comets, a merry chase,
Loyal giggles, in space we race.

A cosmic party through the night,
Where giggles bloom in pure delight,
Astronauts with stories to tell,
In this happy, shining shell.

Universe of Unfathomable Fun

In galaxies where pranks do thrive,
Each starburst brings a smile alive,
Gravity's jokes keep us light,
Floating laughter takes to flight.

Silly aliens in a row,
Tripping over space-time's glow,
Planetary pie fights commence,
In this realm, it all makes sense.

Comets tailing laugh-out-loud,
In cosmic theaters, fun is loud,
Wormholes twist, and tickles fly,
As stardust dances through the sky.

Every swirl is a happy dance,
In this space of endless chance,
Unfathomable joy takes flight,
Join the fun, embrace the night.

Starry-Eyed Chuckles

Amidst the stars, with grins so wide,
Cosmic jesters play and glide,
With every cosmic giggle shared,
A universe where all has dared.

Winking planets wink in glee,
As laughter rolls like waves at sea,
Pulsars pound with rhythm true,
Every heartbeat sings with you.

Jovial echoes bounce and sway,
Turn heaviness to bright as day,
Starry-eyed, we share a jest,
In this cosmic playground, we are blessed.

Galaxies swirl in hilarious dance,
Every moment a giant chance,
To frolic freely, full of cheer,
In this vast expanse, we persevere.

Galactic Giggles

Through the cosmos, chuckles soar,
Where every star opens a door,
To realms of whimsy, joy in stacks,
In space, there's strength in quirky acts.

Silly planets spin in fun,
Comets racing, all on the run,
Puppies in spacesuits leap and tumble,
In this void, no room for grumble.

Asteroids toss moustaches bright,
Giggles bubble in sheer delight,
Starlight shimmers with every grin,
A cosmic hug, under our skin.

In this galactic landscape, we find,
Endless laughter, beautifully designed,
So let's twinkle, tease, and beam,
In this universe, we laugh and dream.

Ecstasy in the Expanse

Amidst the stars, the giggles fly,
Planets dance, and comets sigh.
A cosmic joke, oh what a sight,
Jesters spinning in the night.

Nebulas burst with color bright,
Winking stars, oh what a fright!
Space dust tickles asteroids,
In this vastness, joy never avoids.

Galaxies swirl in merry glee,
Meteors chase, just wait and see.
A universe of chuckles grand,
Silly shadows hand in hand.

In the void, the laughter echoes,
Chasing dreams where stardust flows.
Euphoria in every twinkling light,
A celestial playground, pure delight.

Celestial Snapshots of Joy

Capture moments with a stellar flash,
Planets pose, in a cosmic bash.
Shooting stars wink with delight,
As humor glows in the dark of night.

Galactic spirals, a playful tease,
With every orbit, my heart's at ease.
Nebulae giggle in vibrant hue,
Whispers of joy, a cosmic view.

Asteroids chuckle, a raucous dance,
In this universe, joy finds a chance.
Laughter rolls through the Milky Way,
Silly secrets stars convey.

Take a snapshot, hold it tight,
Memories shimmer, oh what a sight!
The cosmos grins, a radiant show,
In this expanse, let happiness grow.

The Melody of Starlight Laughter

Notes of joy drift through the night,
As starlight sings, oh what a flight!
A symphony of the cosmic cheer,
Every twinkle, a giggle near.

Constellations sway, a radiant dance,
Bouncing off planets, they take a chance.
Chords of brilliance fill the air,
With every note, a whimsical flair.

Galaxies croon in harmonized glee,
Melodies echo, wild and free.
Starlit laughter, bright as day,
In this cosmic choir, we sway.

Come join the fun, let spirits rise,
In the night sky, laughter flies.
The cosmos plays its cheerful tune,
Under the watch of the playful moon.

Quirks of Quasars

Quasars giggle, a radiant jest,
Pulsing light from the cosmic fest.
Each flicker brings a silly cheer,
In the vastness, joy draws near.

Wobbling worlds spin round and round,
In their dance, delight is found.
Funny faces in the cosmic breeze,
Twinkling comets, all here to please.

A universe painted with quirks and quirks,
Astrophysical humor in all its perks.
Galactic pranks that make us beam,
Joining the cosmos in a joyful dream.

So take a moment, gaze afar,
And laugh with light from every star.
In this expanse, let laughter flow,
For in the universe, joy will grow.

Moonlit Merriment

Under the glow of the twinkling sky,
A comet sneezes, oh my, oh my!
Planets dance in a cosmic spree,
While moons giggle from their shady tree.

Asteroids tumble with a clumsy flair,
Wobbling like they haven't a care.
Stars wink in glee, as they overhear,
The whispers of laughter that bring us near.

Galaxies swirl, in their cosmic play,
Trading tickles in a milky way.
Space bunnies hop with a chuckling cheer,
In the warmth of the night, no hint of fear.

Meteor showers turn into a fête,
As humorous tales they reciprocate.
With each twinkle, a giggle ignites,
In this moonlit dance, laughter unites.

The Art of Galactic Joy

Nebulae swirl with bubblegum hues,
Creating giggles in the cosmic blues.
A supernova bursts in a fit of cheer,
While stardust sprinkles, enough to endear.

Comets trade jokes on their speedy flight,
Dancing through darkness, a comical sight.
From Saturn's rings, a chuckle will soar,
As the universe giggles, wanting more.

In the vastness, a jester takes stage,
Tickling the void, turning over a page.
The echoes of laughter stretch far and wide,
As worlds unite in this galactic ride.

Through the cosmos, joy rides the waves,
In the heart of the stars, humor saves.
With each burst of laughter, bright and loud,
The universe forms a quirky, warm crowd.

Smirks Beyond the Stars

In a galaxy where giggles bloom,
Astrophysicists dance with a funny tune.
Gravitational pulls can't hold them down,
As they float above in their merry gown.

Stars toss quips like shooting stars,
While dark matter giggles, hiding in bars.
Each smile shared lights up the night,
Creating a cosmos of pure delight.

Light years traveled through bursts of fun,
Creating a playground, second to none.
Floating on laughter, we twirl and glide,
Through swirling smiles on this joyful ride.

With each twinkle, the universe beams,
Comedic wonders spin into dreams.
In the expanse, where laughter unfurls,
We find our joy in this vast, funny world.

Comedic Constellations

Orion tells tales of his heroic quest,
While Pleiades giggles, barely at rest.
Each star a jest, a radiant beat,
In this nightly show, nothing's discreet.

With Saturn as the ringmaster supreme,
Jupiter laughs in a gas giant dream.
Neptune is chuckling with waves of glee,
As the cosmos bursts forth in unity.

The Milky Way shines with a playful spark,
Where shadows and beams light up the dark.
In spirals of joy, we all take flight,
Through the big top of space, what a delight!

Laughter ecstasy flows through the scene,
As galaxies chat, in moments serene.
In this cosmic circus, with all our friends,
The humor of space is where fun never ends.

Chasing Starlight with a Grin

In the night, we race the beams,
With giggles bursting at the seams.
Twinkling orbs like playful eyes,
Chasing dreams beneath the skies.

Meteors dash with a cheeky flair,
Winking down from high up there.
We skip along on moonlit paths,
Sharing secrets and hearty laughs.

Comets weave through cosmic fun,
A carnival dance, just begun.
Stars tickle us with their bright glow,
Painting the universe just so.

So take my hand, let's run away,
In this gala of night and play.
With every light, our spirits soar,
Together, we'll explore and more!

Cosmic Whispers of Joy

Amidst the planets spinning 'round,
Whispers of joy in silence found.
Asteroids chuckle as they zoom,
In the vastness, there's always room.

Nebulas swirl with colors bright,
Painting the canvas of the night.
We laugh alongside each shooting star,
Creating moments that travel far.

Galaxies spin in a playful tease,
Their spirals dance with whimsical ease.
A frolicsome breeze through the dark,
Each twinkling wink igniting a spark.

So let's embrace this cosmic spree,
With laughter shared, just you and me.
The universe smiles, oh so wide,
In this playground where dreams abide.

Celestial Laughter Echoes

In the realm of starlit cheer,
Celestial echoes draw us near.
We toss our heads back, carefree,
As the universe laughs in harmony.

Planets whirl in a joyous dance,
Life is more than just a chance.
Waves of mirth roll through the sky,
With twinkly stars that flutter by.

Space-time ripples with every jest,
Creating moments that feel the best.
We gather joy in cosmic nets,
Collecting memories, no regrets.

So join the fun, let's spark a light,
In this grand adventure of day and night.
With laughter flying, hearts take flight,
Our souls, a tapestry of pure delight.

Radiance of a Thousand Smiles

Within the cosmos, bright and vast,
A thousand smiles are surely cast.
Each grin a star that lights the way,
Guiding us in joyful play.

Shooting stars weave tales of glee,
As comets dance with jubilee.
In darkened skies, we find our fun,
These shining dots, our spirits run.

Galactic pranks and sunny sights,
Bring laughter through the starry nights.
The universe, a fun-filled ride,
With joy and humor as our guide.

So let us twirl in this delight,
Together painting the endless night.
With radiance shared and smiles wide,
In this cosmic realm, let's take pride.

Aurora's Amusement

In a sky of twinkling lights,
Silly stars begin their plays.
With comets doing cartwheels,
And planets lost in merry rays.

Galaxies spin in laughter,
While moons wear goofy grins.
Echoing cosmic chuckles,
As each new joy begins.

Nebulas dance like children,
With colors bright and bold.
The universe cracks a joke,
As stardust tales unfold.

In this playful expanse,
All worries float away.
With every twirl and spin,
Cosmic glee leads the way.

Bright Horizons of Humor

At dawn, the sun starts to tease,
Spreading warmth with golden beams.
Rays chase away sleepy clouds,
Building joy in waking dreams.

A parade of chirping birds,
Join in on the morning laugh.
Their songs twine with the sunlight,
Crafting joy as their autograph.

Waves crashing on the shore,
Giggle like ticklish toes.
Sea breeze whispers funny tales,
Where laughter freely flows.

As the day leads into night,
Stars begin their prankish spree.
With constellations in a dance,
They wink at you and me.

Radiant Cosmic Pranks

In the depths of space so wide,
Jokes float on celestial tides.
Black holes hide the punchlines well,
Asteroids giggle, can't you tell?

Supernovae burst in jest,
Lighting up the cosmic fest.
While comets zoom and sweep along,
In a whirlwind, they sing a song.

Planets wink as they go round,
With each orbit, humor's found.
Stars create a playful scene,
As laughter spills from skies unseen.

In this funny, vast expanse,
The universe does a happy dance.
With every twinkling, spark, and flash,
The cosmos shares its radiant laugh.

Stellar Smiles

Glowing galaxies spiral wide,
With laughter echoing inside.
Each planet grins, a silly face,
Winking in a merry race.

Astrobiologists, look and see,
Funny shapes in zero G.
Tiny aliens on moonbeams ride,
With playful joy, they take their stride.

Meteor showers twinkle bright,
Like giggles shared in the night.
The cosmos hums a happy tune,
As laughter fills the silver dune.

As dusk falls, stars twinkle high,
With a wink and playful sigh.
In the night sky, joys unfold,
A universe of laughter bold.

Laughter Across the Celestial Bridge

Stars twinkle like eyes, full of glee,
Planets dance in the cosmic spree.
Comets carry smiles, fast and bright,
Sprinkling joy through the velvet night.

Asteroids wobble in playful delight,
While moons play tag, hiding from sight.
Galaxies swirl in a merry chase,
Sharing chuckles in endless space.

Whimsies of the Universe Await

Nebulas bubble like pots of stew,
With colors that giggle, yellow and blue.
Shooting stars whisper silly tales,
Of interstellar cats and moonlit trails.

Orbits wiggle, a spiral of cheer,
Wishing wells of laughter are near.
Planets wear hats, oh what a sight,
Dancing through the shadows of night.

Celestial Giggles

Lightyears stretch with a grin so wide,
As comets skip on the cosmic tide.
Galactic pranks spark hilarity,
Creating chaos, a starry parody.

Jupiter giggles, it's ripe with jest,
While Saturn's rings swirl in a fest.
Eclipsed by humor that circles around,
In the vastness, joy's always found.

Cosmic Whispers

Gravity pulls with a jovial sigh,
While black holes chuckle as they fly by.
Stars share puns in celestial halls,
Echoes of laughter through space calls.

The universe sways in a whimsical trance,
All beings engage in a joyful dance.
With each twinkle, a joke takes flight,
In the wonders of endless night.

Whimsy on the Milky Way

Twinkling stars have silly faces,
They wink and giggle through their places.
A cosmic game of peek and hide,
Where laughter flows, and joy's our guide.

Comets zoom in playful chase,
Astronauts in balloon-like grace.
Planets pop with tunes so bright,
In this dance of pure delight.

Nebulae turn into candy floss,
As rainbows swirl and never toss.
Each quasar tells a funny tale,
In the galaxy where chuckles prevail.

So hold on tight, let glee unfold,
In skies of blue and stardust gold.
With every burst, and every cheer,
Our light year trips are full of cheer.

Jokes of the Universe

Why did the star go to school?
To learn some jokes, and break the rule!
It twinkled bright with laughter shared,
In cosmic halls, no one was scared.

Black holes winked with playful glee,
Pulling giggles from you and me.
A meteor cracked a punchline loud,
Sending waves of joy through the crowd.

Saturn wore a ring of bold bling,
Singing songs of joy, it could swing.
And Pluto, small, with a cheeky grin,
Joined in the fun with a little spin.

So here we spin, in space so wide,
With jokes that make the stars collide.
In the universe, where laughter plays,
Each moment shines in the brightest rays.

Lighthearted Interstellar Dreams

In a rocket made of candy bars,
We zoomed past all the shooting stars.
With giggles as our guiding light,
We danced through loops both day and night.

Alien friends with silly hats,
Joking with the space-time cats.
They bounce around in joyful spins,
Taking bets on who will win.

Galaxies swirl in vibrant hues,
Painting jokes that we all can use.
Floating through this playful scene,
Where every day feels like a dream.

So grab your joy and take a ride,
With twinkling hearts, we'll soar and glide.
In dreams of space, we find our ways,
To chuckle under starlit rays.

Comet's Joyful Dance

A comet twirled with grace and style,
Making loop-de-loops with a cheeky smile.
Its tail, a stream of shimmering light,
Whispered jokes that took flight.

Passing planets joined the fun,
In this cosmic dance, we all run.
With giggles echoing through the void,
Every frown on Earth destroyed.

Nearby moons laughed, clapping hands,
Creating rhythm that surely stands.
Each bounce of joy ignited glee,
As stardust sprinkled joyfully.

So let this merriment stay in sight,
Comets dancing with pure delight.
In this endless space, we find a chance,
To share a laugh in a joyous dance.

Supernova Smiles

In a galaxy wild with glee,
Stars twinkle with a joke or three.
Planets spin in a jovial race,
Asteroids roll with a comic grace.

Nebulas burst with colorful flair,
While comets dance through cosmic air.
Each photon beams with a cheeky grin,
Creating a fiesta where all can win.

Shooting stars share a secret laugh,
As the moon winks, joy at its craft.
Stellar giggles echo and soar,
In this space where fun knows no floor.

Galactic chuckles, a merry spree,
Laughter travels like light, wild and free.
In the cosmos, pure delight,
A universe painted in humor's light.

Dance of the Starry Scouts

Tiny stars in a dizzy swirl,
Galactic giggles unfurl.
With twinkling eyes, they gather round,
Creating joy in the vast profound.

They sway in patterns, a cosmic show,
Wobbling light, a shimmering glow.
Each leap brings laughter, a shimmering tease,
Through the asteroidal, breezy freeze.

A duet of planets sings along,
Harmonizing a whimsical song.
In the vacuum, a playful cheer,
Echoes softly, drawing us near.

With every spin and starry jest,
A vibrant joy within them rests.
As they dance through cycles of night,
In their orbit, pure delight.

Heavenly Humor

Clouds of cotton, soft and bright,
Fluffy giggles fill the night.
Stars play pranks on the wandering moon,
Joking softly, a lonesome tune.

Orbits twist in playful glee,
The cosmos whispers, "Come dance with me!"
Gravity pulls their merry chase,
As time chuckles in zero space.

Solar flares flicker with jest,
Jovial worlds in their cosmic fest.
Lunar humor shines like suns,
In this realm, laughter runs.

A starlit joke for all to share,
In the depths of celestial air.
For in the sky, surprises bloom,
In a universe full of room.

Joy across the Cosmos

The Milky Way's a joyful parade,
With sparkles of laughter that never fade.
Galaxies spin in a whimsical whirl,
Creating a joke for every girl and girl.

Stars play tag in the night so blue,
With comets racing to join the crew.
Every twinkling light's a burst of cheer,
In the vastness where dreams appear.

With echoes of laughter in every zone,
The universe invites us to roam.
In each nook of the celestial sphere,
A smile awaits, a moment dear.

So float through the cosmos, let joy ignite,
In this playful expanse, everything feels right.
Embrace the giggles, let worries depart,
For the universe laughs, a grand work of art.

Radiant Revelry

Stars twinkle with glee, in the cosmic parade,
Jokes tumble through space, where giggles cascade.
Asteroids bounce in rhythm, a silly dance,
While comets burst forth, in a glittery prance.

Planets spin round, in a playful race,
With Saturn's rings wobbling, the silliest grace.
Galaxies swirl, with laughter confined,
In the vastness of space, joy intertwined.

The sun's bright smile casts shadows that sway,
In a carnival of dreams, where whimsy holds sway.
Each cosmic chuckle, a melody light,
Echoes through starlight, a pure delight.

So gather the stardust, and hold it so tight,
In this universe playful, where joy takes flight.
In every corner, a quirky surprise,
For in the vast heavens, humor never dies.

When Nebulas Smile

In the depth of the night, where the stardust twirls,
Nebulas giggle, with colors that whirls.
They flicker and poke at the dark velvet sky,
Spreading laughter like whispers, oh my, oh my!

Supernova shimmers, bursting with cheer,
While black holes chuckle, drawing us near.
A cosmic jest here, a jovial jest there,
Every twinkling star has a story to share.

The moons play hopscotch on beams of the sun,
With giggles and wiggles, they frolic for fun.
Every flicker of light, a twinkling jest,
Across the vast space, a merry conquest.

So follow the echoes of laughter so wide,
Through shimmering starlight, let joy be your guide.
In the galactic embrace, where smiles aren't brief,
Find humor in orbits, oh sweet cosmic relief.

Moonbeams and Merriment

Moonbeams are tickling the edges of night,
Sprinkling laughter, making everything bright.
With shadows that jiggle, and breezes that sway,
Every star joins in for a glorious play.

Twinkling delights, with a wink and a grin,
Shooting stars darting, let the fun begin!
Planets all giggle, spinning round on their axis,
Each one a character, full of fine practice.

Galaxies whirl in a dance of delight,
As comets play tag, dazzling and light.
The universe chuckles, in an endless spree,
In this cosmic carnival, pure jubilee.

So gather your dreams in a silvery net,
With moonlight that sparkles, you're sure to forget.
The worries that lurk, behind every star,
In a realm of enjoyment, just venture afar.

Cosmic Comedy

Cosmic clowns juggling, in the starry expanse,
With meteors rushing, they twirl and they dance.
Galactic giggles bubble, through meteoric lanes,
As planets swap tales of their whimsical gains.

The sun cracks a joke, it's a fiery delight,
While Mercury's winks dart in and out of sight.
With every flare-up, the laughter ignites,
In the theater of night, where fun takes flights.

Asteroids tumble, with comical flair,
Brushing past Venus, with nary a care.
Each cosmic misstep, a laugh in the void,
As stars burst with humor, endlessly buoyed.

So float through the cosmos, where everything's bright,
Join the chorus of chuckles that dance in the light.
A symphony of joy in this vast, endless dome,
In the comedy of cosmos, we'll always be home.

Smiles that Span the Universe

In the vastness, giggles soar,
Stars twinkle back with a playful roar.
Comets trail in a bright parade,
While planets wink in a cosmic charade.

Nebulas swirl, a canvas of cheer,
As moons chuckle, feeling near.
Galaxies twist in a silly embrace,
Creating majesty with a joyful face.

Photon rays dance with a jolly flair,
Bringing laughter to the galaxy's air.
Gravity pulls, but humor lifts free,
In the tapestry of space, hilarity we see.

Asteroids bounce with a jolly sound,
While the universe spins, joy all around.
Every star is a smile, bright and bold,
In this cosmic jest, laughter unfolds.

Whirlwind Whimsy in the Cosmic Dance

In the cosmic prelude, where giggles ignite,
Stars tango in shoes of pure light.
Dancing planets, they twirl and swirl,
Each rotation a chuckle, a joyful whirl.

Gravity hums a silly tune,
As constellations wiggle under the moon.
Shooting stars race, with laughter in tow,
Painting the night with a whimsical glow.

Black holes tease with a playful grin,
Like cosmic jesters, they pull us in.
In this whirlwind of orbit and spin,
The universe giggles; let the fun begin!

Asteroids giggle, the meteors cheer,
As cosmic clowns drift, drawing near.
In the dance of the heavens, delight takes flight,
With a whirlwind of whimsy, through day and night.

Joyful Starlings in Infinite Skies

Under starlit whispers, mischief awakens,
In every constellation, laughter is shaken.
Joyful starlings in a soaring spree,
Darting through the cosmos, wild and free.

Galactic giggles paint the air bright,
As comets fly past with a wink of delight.
Nebulas puff up like fluffy clouds,
Wrapping the universe in laughter loud.

Shooting stars dash, fulfilling a wish,
With every twinkle, a cosmic swish.
In the expanse's embrace, we feel so light,
As joy spirals boldly, taking flight.

From quasar to quasar, the chuckles flow,
In this infinite dance, we watch the show.
The universe giggles, a symphony vast,
In the joyful starlings, our spirits are cast.

Grin Unfurled Across the Galactic Plains

On galactic plains where the light beams play,
A grin unfolds, brightening the day.
Quirky krakens and starry-eyed fish,
Swirl in the cosmos, floating with a wish.

Celestial creatures share stories anew,
In this open expanse, join in the view.
Cosmic critters dance in a merry parade,
As laughter erupts in a joyful cascade.

In this universe vast, a tapestry spun,
Where every laugh is a new, bright sun.
Galaxies shimmer with a playful embrace,
Pressing joy deep in the fabric of space.

As stardust sprinkles from comets that race,
We find our own humor in this boundless place.
With grins unfurled, we wrap up the night,
In the galactic fields, everything feels right.

www.ingramcontent.com/pod-product-compliance
Lightning Source LLC
Chambersburg PA
CBHW051655160426
43209CB00004B/908